ABOUT THE AUTHOR

Work rooted in word-witchery and the working class, **Louise Fazackerley** is a poet from the exotic Northern streets of Orwell's Wigan. In performance she explores the synergy between poetry and movement. Her socially conscious writing makes the ugly beautiful and the mundane fantastical.

Winner of the BBC Radio New voices award, Louise is signed to Nymphs & Thugs spoken word label where she released two audio books- *Love Is A Battlefield* and *Bird St.* Her collection *The Lolitas* is the subject of 'Love Is A Rebellious Bird' an installation and film work by international artists AL + AL. She recently supported punk poet legend Dr. John Cooper Clarke on his sold-out tour.

Louise is a director at Write Out Loud, a national organisation supporting grass roots poetry and currently poet-in-residence at Lily Lane Primary School. She is a highly experienced workshop leader, facilitating in education, prison and community settings. You may have seen or heard her on BBC 1, BBC Radio 3,4,5 or read her blog in The Guardian Northerner.

Louise Fazackerley
The Lolitas

VERVE
POETRY PRESS
BIRMINGHAM

PUBLISHED BY VERVE POETRY PRESS
https://vervepoetrypress.com
mail@vervepoetrypress.com

FIRST PUBLISHED DEC 2019

Printed and bound in the UK
by Imprint Digital, Exeter

ISBN: 978-1-912565-36-8

*This book is dedicated to my
strong and passionate Mum
and to my kind, clever
daughters
Frank and Bella.*

CONTENTS

INTRODUCTION

The Lolitas speak back sharply to their Nabokovian silences in this outstanding first poetry book by Louise Fazackerley. Written from the perspectives of both child and mother, what you are about to read is an unflinching archive of lyric poems and memories made to spin into the present and echo the past. Threaded together by an exceptional series of 'Spokes', the reader eavesdrops on the world where young Lolita (recast as Lola) grows up watching Humbert. Watching him, watching back.

> *There's this lad across the backs and I fink he's watching me.* His window was on the next spoke, higher up than ours. *There's these flashes of light. I fink he's got binoculars or summat to see me really good.*

Written in solidarity with the #MeToo movement, confronting difficult themes from sexual abuse to underage grooming, Fazackerley takes on those who remain at large and nameless beyond the known and reprehensible (the Epsteins, Trumps, Weinsteins, Prince Andrews—'The moon says Prince Andrew is the world's most protected N.O.N.C.E'). This is a series of poems we as readers—as human beings no less—*need* to read. Not many poetry books can claim this essential presence and vitality whilst critiquing patriarchy. Taking on what legal frameworks on sexual assault (with their binary codes of perpetrator/victim, etc.) still fail to recognise . In an excellent Introduction to *Where Freedom Starts: Sex Power Violence #MeToo*—a recent downloadable 'report' from Verso books—Jessie Kindig rightfully lambasts the law as not being able to fully recognise 'the undisciplined nature of desire and sex nor the systemic violence of capitalism, white supremacy, patriarchy.' Fazackerley picks much of this apart by interrogating ideas around sexuality, sexual development and sexual abuse amid dailiness and ritual (chatroom to bar to bedroom). This is a radical, working class poetry coming from the estates of Wigan, in the North West of England, where Fazackerley was raised and lives now. Voicing those who might often be denied voice in speaking back to sexual abuse, Fazackerley speaks through her characters, bringing them to life:

> She drew her bony little self in her pink cotton knickers and triangle bra. *This is arty, right. Not dirty or anything. There's loads of nudies in art because the human body is gorgeous. You'd be like a sexy Botticelli or summat, if you was in art.* The angle of sight, from his window to hers, meant he probably couldn't see her. Or maybe he could.

She evokes social issues in relation to sexual awareness and class discrimination, lack of education on sexuality, but also covers BREXIT in relation to her central theme:

> remain/ leave, the same
> things happen to you
> and you and you and you

For me, poetry has to have the appearance of music in it. Fazackerley is a poet of both voice and hearing in these poems and sequences. Her ear is tuned up, creating sonic nuance and discord. She has perfect pitch. The more obvious *message* approach would presumably be to speak *literally* or *directly* to her central theme. Fazackerley dares to try something else. Her simultaneous propulsion and disruption of narrative/image creates an atmosphere, a tension. Sound shifts, coheres, de-coheres time and again, revealing the organics of thought, its silences and revelations. Fazackerley is easily able to flit between modes—performance to experimental—making these poems sing.

'Emerging poet' is, I find, always a reductive term and it doesn't apply here. This is an impressively formed book, from a dedicated writer who has been listening to these constellatory voices for years. Who has *waited* to write it out until they were good and ready. It's a bit of a catchphrase to say this is one of the most impressive debut collections in years, but that's precisely what *The Lolitas* is. To read this book through is to want to read it again.

Importantly, whilst reading this, for me, it was interesting to note that Humbert—whilst being the main character in Nabokov's *Lolita*—is something of an undercard (cue Eryk, a 'Dirty Bertie'). He's someone talked *through* by the lives of the women he surveilles. He's the threat in the air. Ultimately, in its striving for empowerment and transcendence, *the Lolitas* is a tender and deeply intimate book exploring the mother/daughter relationship, wondering as it does, how do we grow up under *his* gaze? How to live on, fully grown?

James Byrne, Edge Hill University, November 2019

The Lolitas

Second Sight

not yet not yet not yet

the world spins ≤ Right

this second chance child
defies the ~~law~~ lore
  nature/ nurture?
she is not the same

it's not the first time

my oddball,
scrawpy, ferocious, fey,
delicious fiend
is disinterested
  in pleasing me

watchful she/ she
        creeps round corners
sucking a sodden thumb

hums in miss-diss-dis-chord
looks left
while the mothers sleepwalk
our eyes wide shut

she stands on chairs

we

sit

down

gob-stoppered

distorted the black mirror ripples
    in her Alice-in-Winterland gaze

I breathed life
into this dollDolores
this Alice, this Eve,
this Lilith, this Lolita,
this Gretel, this Greta
of mine

she is
no-one's
marionette

robust, still
she does not
yet fret, ~~fearful,~~ I
creep round corners
        to watch her
watching
sucking that
sodding, sodden thumb

stoppering the worlds
        she cannot speak

Spoke 657: Zero

Lola's bedroom. A back room. *It's a screwin matchbox, Ma.*

A line from an ancient 2020 *post-punkpoetz* podcast flaps round the room and my head, like a flat lightsphere reflecting from the face of a watch. *Why did you have to mek us grow up here?* Last year Lola's Ma tried to fix it up a bit for them. When she was still cheap and cheerful. You could get sick wallplastic from the scrappies. *Knockety knock! Delivery for unit 5.*

Lola's Ma's string arms measuring with someone's tape she borrowed. Lola's Ma's string arms cutting with the paint spattered scissors. The neon wallplastic getting stuck on her thistle hair and . stuck to itself. *Oh Ma! Yer makin a mess of it. Let me help. Let me help.*

Smooth the bubbles. Lola, white and only a few burns, coz kids don't hardly ever go out these days, not kids like us anyway. B.F.F.'s got dollops of Flatline and SkankyBlush caked into the carpet. Greasy, squashed lumps of make-up, make it, moon bursts, ring worm you can't get out. *You're a trollop Alice. You're a trollop Lola. Girls! Stop saying trollop.*

You're a trollop Ma. Someone should invent a better remover. The slices of wall around the rectangular mirror, with white bulbs screwed into its edge, a palette of fingerprint. The pair of them trying to get ultra-close to themtrueselves.

Bunk beds. Stars white-tacked to the ceiling. Lola on top, Ma on the bottom. At night- an earbud each, the screen buzzing, the wire stretched taut.

Spoke 657: Dance Monkey Dance

Whiskey, battery acid, neat. *I'm honestly struggling to believe they're throwing money away down here. What about the transport links?* Eryk was getting on Lola's Ma's tits. Carts dunt count as a transport link. Tracks grew like dandelions. Walking's not that safe down here. Falling off the edge. We wuz sitting in the doorway. *Oy, grumpy!* Lola smirking coz we know Eryk wears Cuban heelstackers to look a bit taller. You can't wear your shoes in the front room in Lola's unit. Lola's Ma talking like full-fat Coke. *We're an Official roll-out pilot area, babe. I'll show you the email. See! 'Success 321.' Hi ho, hi ho, it's off to work you go. No, it's not a work initiative. It's something for the kids. It's population control- that's what it is. Not enough babies being born coz no fricker actually sees each other anymore. Frickin Authority socio-manipulation. That's what you get when mutual masturbation is on the curriculum and HomePawnMaker is bankrolled by Virgin.*

You've never complained before, Eryk.

There'd been a frickin bad buzz building for weeks. Not just on the Authority memes, poking up in between lessons on the Achieve Hub. Even on a shitty pirate stream me and Lola found. Bingo. An actual 3D fullonphysical Social Hub was going to be re-opened on a spoke near us. Awkward right?

Scent

spelling tests to Saturday night smashed he tries to _____
you spare land ciderlight train tracks on teeth ping pong pissed
the scrub is a waltzer he tackles you your hips spin-the-bottle
wtf smashed to the ground he WWF's you sex is sport he tries to
_____ you you are nothing skin cells on glass too scared
to call to spectacled friends atoms he'd kill them he is a black hole
can't fit his thick hands down your babyfat jeans scrubber you're
used to fighting scrape yourself upright
walk it off

bemygirlfriend bemygirlfriend

he strayDoberman

tracks you
two miles home

the only time you hope a car will _____ *stop*

stop you say *stop it*
yes you say
deal with him in maths on Monday
in the safety of the teachers reach
no shit on the doorstep for your Mum to bleach

_____

Answers: finger, f*ck, kiss, stop

Spoke 657: Tom Cat

There's this lad across the backs and I fink he's watching me. His window was on the next spoke, higher up than ours. *There's these flashes of light. I fink he's got binoculars or summat to see me really good.*

Shuddup Lola. Why does she always think they're watching her? Sometimes Lola read her book, full sat up to the window and left it propped, for when she wasn't in the bedroom, so he could see what she was reading. Sometimes she sat on the floor in the corner, in front of a mirror propped against the wall. She drew her bony little self in her pink cotton knickers and triangle bra. *This is arty, right. Not dirty or anything. There's loads of nudies in art because the human body is gorgeous. You'd be like a sexy Botticelli or summat, if you was in art.* The angle of sight, from his window to hers, meant he probably couldn't see her. Or maybe he could. I sat on Lola's Ma's bottom bunk out of the way. Two little ducks. Yak, yak, yak.

Playing Rounders

grass shouldered, the orange
brick wall at my back, scratchy
as sought-after stubble

flamingo-legged
I lean, 13
trying to be smaller

apple-head Adam
his bowl-cut
beatnik straight

first base, not base
my brace bursts the bubble
and the lip of his peachy face

every night after that
like suction cups
we're stuck together

chewing gum arms
in the waltz position
tilted heads

he goes away,
kayaking with his sink school,
two burnt-pink weeks in the Ardeche

his boyish, buoyant postcard
navigates the stars
too late sucker, sucker punch

                              I cop with
Dear John, his best mate, the back stop

    love and other indoor sports
                              L xxx

Round 1

She's at his house

party, drinking moonmilk, 15,

and he instructs her to go outside

leans her against the wall

like an unopened umbrella.

(*a/s/l?*)

Let Me Be Your Fantasy

He has been her coach

since she was 11.

She is tiny, tin-ribbed,

has a nose like a handle

or a beak, she thinks

I can't believe he fancies me.

(34, male, Manchester)

He _____ her.

Spoke 657: Your Plug-in

Scrappies shouting at the front of the house. *A plug-in for the weekend, ladies and gentlemen.* You had to ask Mo, in bean can 3, to look through his window if you wanted to see anything happening at the front of the house and *stay safe.* Once, once upon a curfew, a cart came off the lines and took the corner of a house out- two of the downstairs units inside got big holes in. They're still tarped up now. Once upon a daytime, two Meth heads running up the street with one trying to stab the other with this cranking great huge knife. All the neighbours were out watching- better than Netflix. Didn't know there were so many people on our spoke. It come on the Crime Hub and everything. The spoke got yellow-taped off for about a week. *Fame at last for 657.*

Quarry

british houses printed   clack clack
clack   our estates
manufactured
  monopoly properties
houses nobody made
the front doors all the same
  vast headscarves of land
stretched across a jam jar of carbon-earth
anthracite worm-roads
rot underneath
a construct and living on
concrete
snowflake
floats

        *

foal me, 1992, acne mushrooms
  an underpass of cardboard walls
beneath my bridge-damp fringe
foetal, sweating, the dull
doctor does a home
  Debbie Does Denton
visit, *do you think
you could be pregnant?*

my singular mum
potential explosion, mental
-ly ill, 28, stick insects on
privets in a Flying Saucers tub
picker packer
picker packer
fat, factory, softly
she's only 12
Doctor

*

*** Selkirk Grove
Norley Quarry
Wigan
WN5 9XY

*

fly a cyclone kite hope
we assemble for free at
the hexagonal library they
let us take five books at
a time 1984 it looks

like a conservatory
or the T.A.R.D.I.S.
  the ~~kit~~ kite that is a plastic
Morrisons carrier
black wool milled through
the handles baa baa
wind bag

they fill the open-pit
their share of sunk cars
a milk bottle from 1944
newspapers, and killing stones
a fucking Leachate swimming pool

*

poppet me, sapling, ivy strangling
my thighs, lolloping
Comet Road
  gentleman GP smokes
  in his missionary hut
  outpost on Marsh Green
  it looks like a potting shed

grafters Punch-andJudy-ing
geriatric queuechain methane
wildflower me
statistic makers, you
pluck us over like weeds
hareseed in rabbit's clothing
production pills

*

remain/ leave, the same
things happen to you
and you and you and you
the Holy Doctor tells us
13, 14, 15,

we're lying
we're too young, imbecile
refuses to give
us birth
/control

Stroboscope

black moon

My grandma left me an empty jam jar.
In the clearing up and out,
I saved all the salt sachets
she'd stolen from the bingo
and bought myself an addict.
He didn't replace the one we'd lost
but I knew she'd approve.

*

I'm not big enough to hold
his huge head,
the size of a small planet. I bought
myself, a monochrome

Is that a comet in your trackies
or are you just pleased to see me?

Wish upon an extinguished
star for advancement in medical
technology so his hair will grow again.
Who ever heard of a moon with hair?
We are *two grand* too grand for those things.

I get to be an astronaught.

*

body tide

your head, the shape of it,
a big brick of coke, the size you transport in a sports hold-all
like a decapitation in the back of a car with false plates,
one careful owner, Brum to New Liverpool,
the shape of a bent knee, a balled fist, a pinata

*

The sky in our bathroom is landlord white.
I shower and count the constellation of squashed flies.
What happened to them?
They look like abjads
escaped from a typebar.
I don't know this old language.

*

My grandma would hug starmen, saints and strangers.

*

The black, cracked bucket in the backyard
left over from last cycle.
We are lazy decorators.
there's sugar in wallpaper paste
You, squatting like a man in a Bangkok trok.
I watch through the patio doors,
an observatory,
you, Neanderthal browed,
stick in hand, stir a rainvisc cordial.

Something swims.

*

blood moon

black moon, bad apple
while you slept
someone laid a dog hide upon you
you rolled out of the bed damp
onto all fours, frightening me
a forest floor of creased clothes

I lived with it, the stranger, for ten days
it is nocturnal
only a paperchain of earth, rolled and lit
connects one to the other

*

A late pregnancy.
Nothing has hatched.

*

the constellations won't stop following us
we have gravitas

Saturday morning in bed
dust motes disco space dust

February motorway snow
rolls in like Star Wars

even the migraine of fleas
on the cat could be Hercules M13

*

hunger moon

We honeyquick to Prague.
The night sky concave.
Underneath, yellow stims,
the hundreds and thousands you put in your tea
when the sugar runs out.

*

a tracer of salt
all the people are white
I know I'm psychic
let's not talk about the electric impulses now
we need to talk about the baby mosquitoes in the bucket

did you kill them?

*

burnt caramel freckles on your shoulder

*

in your sea the C in the bulbous milk cranium
the o in the golden iris
m other Russia nostrils- fox fur-lined trapper's hats
the m in the Andes of your plum upper lip
the violent bow of a bottomdweller u
know/ no/ n
ist ist ist

I get to be Atlas

*

wolf

monochrome moon
Today you went to the doctors,
your ego squashed in the surgery,
hoping for Better Pills.
You were prescribed questions

             artistic spack
spicknspamhead
             automote
0 1 0 1
condition
             bullshit spectrum
stringstrungup
             axis disorder

describe sadness

The label itches.
add to addict
  my Grandma's three wishes
father, lover, lune

we wait

*

Spoke 616: Slick

The rats the kids run have some Synth in them. So, like, nearly a metre, toe to tip, some of em. *Whippety whip, ass lickers!* Adum's best fighter is called Binjuice. *BIN JUICE! BIN JUICE!* They're all big but Binjuice is bigger. The rumour is, if you could get a Mam who was breast-feeding to sell you a bitto the squeezed-out-stuffing, that milk was like rocket fuel for rat-muscle. *O course there's Mams who sell it.* Just living, trying to be alive, trying to live, to stay africkinglive, costs a lot. Here and everywhere I reckon. Adum brushes its teeth with a tiny toothfile to help keep em from growing too long. And to stop it scissoring through and running off. Brick. Metal. Bits of the yellow Texas polycarbon Arc that'd fell down. Protect us from the sun and the falling burnstuff. *I just want you be safe little Binners.* Sedative in the ice-cream. Dunno if it's a girl or a boy. It's hard to keep em caged. And short, sharp teeth help with The Maimings. *Slice and dice!* There's not much glory down here but running a top sewer is AWESOME.

Kawaii

fur baby false-baby
coat like sastrugi
ears Alpines my fingers ski
      your brittle skull

little pet vermin
whiskers antennae
you do not watch TV
days/dreams

4am falsetto
my breast cage
the pianoforte paddle of paws
drill-musician

toe-biter
hamsterhorrorflick
me Schrodingerish

I'm sorry for saying *I'll eat you*
I'd eat you on a butty

Spoke 669: Villain

Adum had got Binjiuce off of Humbert, from his spoke, when he was about 10. That was when Humbert was still selling em, before he shut all the young lads and pusses off and started hiding away. Beats tripping up from his cellar unit. Humbert looked like a cross between a sewer rat himself and a ripped armchair. Black stuffing crawling up from under his vest onto his neck to meet his slicked back hair. I never seen Humbert in a sewt. It was always vests and trackies. No track marks. On your marks. The birds loved him. Flock of Mams flouncing up and down in the Backs, past his lean. Pretending they was checking on their brats. A hip-swaying, wet-lipped slow-mo race. It's hard to look sexy in a sewt. *He's making me sweat just perving at him. He's washing his hair in Virile, him. Thought that was banned?* Rumour was Humbert was a bit of a Dirty Bertie.

Stupor

peel the smashed wasps
from the windscreen
scrape them half wet
into the glove box
they buzz
I get two parking tickets today

my ex cancels Christmas
you offer to take his
place so I can go out
to a 40th with Rachel
from Social Services

we return at 1am
can of Coke zero for you
your pupils are pins
jaundiced whites

one of my kids is reading
as you slur words and
fly into door frames

the daffodils we did not plant
in bright wellies in the dirtyard
hard-faced as weed
fucking stupid I get it
trumpet in my sleep

A Word in Your Shell-like, Babe

listen to piss and vinegar's Bank Holiday siren

that down-turn spun cone, like a Kiss Me Quick
mussel man spilling kids, hard as scratchings,
                              in the crease of the pram,
they're fishing pier-crusted arches
                              for bogeys, salt prizes to lick,
this Mam, rum as a donkey, high-kicks and splits

pay day loans stack as stilts,
she's a maybeMILF, silt showgirl, free guilt
clown-face, the spangly costume nearly fits

the penny slot tilts, this Mam, stretchmarks sand-spilt,
she slip-steps, wildly swims the mollusc womb
splashed, breathed, driftwards
rides Neptune

at first light, the sea strathspeys
don't go back to work on Tuesday

Private/s

In the back room of The Red Tent
we watch *Women Who W*nk*
and each   other, blushing
inside, *you are o l d*
spells the witchbrightchild
on stage, dress of washed blood, pushing

us to say the word   wank. This audience won't
talk   masturbation *shy?* teenage daughters
why not? fools the fire-lit comedy clit *don't*
you want her to be Venus?

                        I'm sort of
scared of making a show of myself.   One
mum says, 'I thought she'd find it out herself.'
In the same way, we just find out that
carrots   are good for

making us see in the dark.

W*nk finishes in a climax, and guilt, obviously.
Jokester. Fiddler. Meddler.

And if I was a good parent I'd

<u>To do</u>
stop/start beating around the bush
audition the finger puppets
make a Pussy Play Masterclass
er, for the kids. *(oh, oh)* Awks.

Her head pokes through
the hood of her frock.

She's peeping through
the laughing stocke.

She cartwheels.
Ta-Da!
        In the bar, she whispers
I'm the double o in the fool.

Her fingers and thumbs
make binoculars.

Spoke 657: Call Me

*Call me Charlie when we're on a Public chat. I don't look old enough to be
your Mam, thank you.* She's a right deltahead sometimes. *I'm going
out IRL on Friday night. He's taking me to a Real Rain Experience. He's
got clearance for The Hub.* So fricking what.

Lola is not LOLS. Lola's mad coz her Ma asked me to follow her.
Slit-eyed I watch her roll out her bed and land on all four paws.
Padding out, past me on the floor, past my lean, into the backs.
She won't tell me who she's meeting. *I'm just going learning dancing.
Someone's teaching me.* Tongue dancing more like. *I'm not telling you
coz you like mi Ma better than me.* She doesn't mean it. *Just coz you've
no Ma of your own.* Lola's Ma wishes we was lesbians so neither of
us get cock-knocked up dead young. *Even lesbians hit each
other, Ma.*

I become the night. Just coz I'm fat doesn't mean I can't become
the night and sneak after her. She's a-visiting the rat-man.

*Have a good time. Don't worry about us. Love you M...I mean, Charlie.
Bye Eryk.*

Bye Alice. Love you Dolores, my little Lola doll.

Consumer

I bought a new dress

In the fitting room, my child, 11
Gently rounds her hand, my tummy

Mam, it's a little food baby.
When is it due?
When you diet?

I bought

a new daughter

Costume Designer - Urgent

Words to fit

bitch	coquette	faunet
flirt	harpy	imp
jailbait	lolita	nymph
nymphet	nympho	nymphomaniac
psycho	psychobitch	psychokiller
quesquecest	scratchanitch	siren
slut	sylph	underage
urge	virgin	witch

Spring

darling, complete the crossword below

Horizontal:

2. softbrownpuppybodies
3. Name another place pale pubescent girls can be started at in perfect impunity remindful of that granted on in dreams.
5. What do you call a deadly little demon amongst the most wholesome of children?
7. What should girls do?
8. Are all children nymphets?

Vertical:

1. Who is the main character in 'Lolita'?
4. Name one place pale pubescent girls can be started at in perfect impunity.
6. Is Chapter 5 the only place to find information on nymphets?

Ofcoursenot Orphanage School Yes Taboo Humbert Humbert nevergrownup Nymphet

Round 2

(self interview)

bruise, the colour of, and delineation of, a burn
at training you saw the buckle mark
on the soft, white belly of his son
serpent you did
nothing
the boy, 8

you said *yes*
you enjoyed having sex with him
hard-faced nymphet
on tape, the interview red-taped
skipping rope spooled to the virgin bed
XTC, *this is normal right?*

your square parents
left you, 11, in his corner
bought you the blue shorts
the white vest the red gloves
surely she's safe
with her instructor

off your head you said *he made me*
apple teacher kid
feel so good about myself
punch the bag
you, 15, this does not count
as statutory rape in the UK in 1994

where is he in this?

Round 3

she lies on her back
judge her
cockroach wings digging dirt
in the ~~victim~~ boxer's holding cell

me, the Alice, her corner man,
 youdidnothingwrong
I'm rubbing her thighs
with Tiger Balm
in a long-sleeved high neck blue dress
that is professional looking and comes past my knees
with brightly flying
birds on it- the
sort I wear for
parent's evenings
-the one I choose
to wear to court

I know where you live

she's been training, trying
to slough off the stunted
skin he grew her in

who needs sleep anyway?

she can run round his circus whip instead
she jumps through hard paper hoops
makes babies with a man her own age

opiate, she holds up her firstborn as offering
bless me Father for I have sinned
cognitive dissonance
burns like brown
he denies everything
says there was nothing
nothing between them
nothing?

11 - 23
1990-2003
R.I.P.

H.R.H
embroidered in hemp
on his Thai-silk robes
head bobbing, 66
kill-cocky

waiting amateurs score this
a split decision

waiting, we know
we are the teachers now

Spoke 669: The Hanged Man

Humbert skidded into his cellar. Kafka's abortion. Door slam.
Walls heaving with blood-purple vines and fancy rat babies
pressing their soft snuffle snouts up to the plastic viewing area.

Outside, lads were finding holes to push thin rods in. Dads and
Mams and owd biddies egging them on. Whoop-de-wa-wa-wa.
They're getting to serve up some illegal batches of chemical fear
and everybody is fricking loving it. Mob mentality, baby. Squirt
some faux-cheese on the lenses of the little eyes/Eyes. Skillz.
Humbert will be a fricking Guy Fawkesio.

Dir Tee Pig. Dir Tee Pig.

There's no way the Authority are going to intervene. All the way
out here to quell a bit of lynching? Not fricking likely.

Spoke 657: Rebreather

Lola's Ma's boyfriend. The latest. Probably not the last. Less creepy than the last one. Uncle Eryk taught literacy on one of the slum-hub sites. His potato nose- a red web of wires. Eryk slouched on their couch in the living room in the flat. One burgundy stripey sock and one blue Nike one. Classy, Eryk. Cheesefoot. Just do frick all. Wearing a soft, collapsible, camel blazer, height of fashion ten years ago, but it weren't working proper coz when her took his sewt off, the shoulders didn't re-inflate. *Eryk, you don't noffink look like your photo on the Achieve Hub.*

He don't look nowt like his picture on the Eroti-Hub either, babe. Lola's Ma snorting fizzy wine out her nose and then trying to pull it together and keep her face dead straight. Lola smirking. Old spudhead, his gaze sliding between them, blank. Facial expressions were out of fashion for those trying to move up in the world. You could tell he'd had a good education.

Step

a stream of Mam's boyfriends parade like the pink elephants in
Dumbo and this one reads you Blyton at bedtime and this one
scoops you from an avocado-green bathroom floor, your hair spun
seaweed, your polyester nightgown, you smell of charity shop and
chip butty vomit, this one paints your bedroom fingernail-black,
the whitetoothpastesmile stripes a beat of love the size of a
starling's heart, while the window cleaner makes a peepingTom
porthole, asks if you support Newcastle United and everyone
round here knows, this is a revolving room

man sized, the doors in this house are too small for him, he keeps
hitting his moon head, the doors in this house are for girls, he's got
stuck inside us, Alice unlaughing at his Dad jokes, Lola singing,
inside of you the Eye rotates 360 degrees, is the moon a
N.O.N.C.E? you discuss the existence of the Eye, you and the
moon, who is remarkably well read, even though you are sure,
sure-ish, that the man in the moon is a myth, like happy families

you take the moon to a school play, he falls asleep, the species of
birdsong you are growing is unknown to you, are you stupid/safe?
the moon is feeding them seeds of Thatcher and #thuglife and
this light is both iridescent and commonplace, you imagine, Alice
strokes his head, *common-law fatherling*, sweet crater faces- all three
of them, a Russian roulette of your boyfriends, one small step,
landing

Net

she swims to school, *RUN!*
the black frill bobbing

waistband rolled like a stick of rock
warm-blooded, normal not frigid

bet I was a sexy baby
   coz I came out naked

her hands gangnam style
gangly, she does a booty twerk

sun in the eye of the child

     backstroking

tadpole traffic in ties
the 657 bus, a public pool
flash flood of flesh

little belt-ers
     legs, 11

the length of them
toothpick pins

throw sin
   catch rodmen, fishing

Science

boys laugh
girls with their hands over petri dish faces

ungainly as lambs
heads too big, eyes boggle

everyone said Simon was just
looking at the woman's bits
not the baby
being born

vulva I say
vagina I say

before videos young human mammals
worked out what to do

fairytale graveyards folk song story
whispers hand-drawn porn woods

shame
shame?

no shame Simon says
I wuz JUST LOOKING AT HER BITS

science
EXPLODES

girls laugh
boys with hands hiding bunsen burners

First/Thirst

what use is a diagram of a stamen
compared to that rubbery gear stick

walnut whips jellyfish melon-choly

why do boys
more than a handful is a

   32DD
   popcorn eager- she's decided
       to ask him
       her first date.

why do #notallmen think that
nipples are like knobs on a cooker
you twist, I shout

bored, let him practise
opening a bra one-handed
he's still waiting for his applause

do they still call them bases?
   At school she's set 5 in PE.
maybe she'll trip on his trainers
and elbow him in the Fanta

Her father *what is wrong with him*
called him a
'young Keanu Reeves'
tear in his eye

In the car on the way to
   the pictures
   I try to warn her.

Mum, I'm only 12.

L is for …

your daughter, luminous,
a particular sun-demon.

Spells, slant,
Grandma-green eyes.
She compels L.O.V.E. lovely

young mis-witch
of dinosaur and dragon.
She still plays with dolls.

She's got something to tell you
I don't like lads.
Breaks the circle of salt.

Her bedroom is as toy-cluttered
as the mountain range of pus
across her high cheekbones.

We call these cheeks
the Collins apples.

She's coated in cat fur.
Mummy, I'm the L in the L.G.B.T.

You feel some hurt.
Groom greasy hair.

You're unsure why?
You sharpen your claws.

This kid has been going to PRIDE
since she was 5.

And if the rainbow inverted
becomes misery, mad
you will bite
the mealy-mouthed mutts
who spite behind her in R.E.

You do not say to her
Darling, you're only 12.

Confidence Control System

full-fat 14, I was a St. John Fisher
of young men. In my diary
baiting lists with brutal force,
K.I.S.S.I.N.G. dexterity,
systematically
I marked them
out of 10.

Stu	7	a bit sloppy	18, apprentice paint and decorator

acid house DJ and drug-dealer
The romance of it all.
he wanted to come in for a cup of
get your mum onside
tigerstripe iris, catfish, white lies

keyhole
me n Emz n Caz scrawl
the tin street lamp like a scrunchie,
practise French kissing an open can of Coke
sharp tongued
whose catholic small c whose catholic wet-dream is this?

Dabby	6	for a bet	Baz's 13th birthday party
Daz	6.5	for a bet	Baz's 13th birthday party
Dane	9	FAF*	Baz's 13th birthday party

Jamie	2	like snogging a washing machine

Adam   8.5   ♡♡♡   the closest I'll ever get to Kurt
                                                  Cobain

                      When I accidently-let-him-read-my-diary
                            dump him
                            he threw his packet of Polos at me
                                  one mint-with-the-hole at a time

* Fit As F*ck

R.A.P.E.

I told him I was only 15

Spoke 657: Fishing

We eyeball the avatars on the Achieve. Swipe left. Worm CGI bodies and human photo faces. *No way are they making us do Compulsory Community Dancing at the Social Hub. They are. It says right here. It's not dancing- it's a Social, Physical and Mental Wellbeing Training module. The only dancing I know is the sort mi Ma used to do before she got into making money from makeovers. Who'd spend credits on your flat chest?* Cue bedroom catwalk a la Beauty Pageant. *Get your ass out of my face Lola. You stink of fish.* CHA CHA cha-cha-cha. Strictly Come Povs. Dosey-doe and back in your box. *If this Training is compulsory all the kids round here'll be there. Including him what's watching me. Who do you think it is?* There's nearly two thousand kids enrolled with our hub from all over the place and no-one allowed their real name until you're 21. Lola mostly does Art/Graphic/Film modules coz they're free. Science modules are pure credits. *I hope it's RhettBigler. He's hysterical.*

How old do you reckon he is?

Spoke 657: Winterland

You girls have never been that cold. Ha ha ho.

Lola's Ma had a bag full of woollen tights leftover from when it used to get cold at winter. When we're older and we get fellas or birds and they treat us make *sure they frickin treat you, or get out of there- get them to take you to a Real Snow Sesh.* She's saying this while she's cutting the tights up and making them into syfties. She sells them at Christmas. Lola's got this amazing stripey one. It's peachy and pinky and Babycham blue. The leg makes a body and she cuts it again and again to make little legs, all sewed up and little arms, all sewed up. And she twists lastic round the body to make a little flat head. And cuts and sews some pointy triangle ears on- like some of the dats and cogs have got. *Them ears look like your boobs. Shut up Eryk. He shouldn't speak to me like that Ma!*

Lola's Ma is in the other room getting ready. Me and Lola are just chilling when he rolled his soft self up. He plants himself on the sofa, nearly touching Lola. She pulls her knees into her, so she doesn't have to make skin contact with his stinking sewt.

The Hidden

1.

Dad, incarcerated, for raping
her older, half-sister
S, 14, *just like him*
Tokyo
likes: singing, fashion, spag bol
dislikes: female members of staff, fish

she is the first kid in care
I, 21, ever looked after unloved
little sister, Emergency Respite
S played cards with LF
S wrote a letter to Dad

S would like to go to street dance
with LF (carer) next week
half-undressed
I saw Sarah at night in the street.

Schoolgirls for Sale
read *The Daily Mail article*
club Kurione, Akihabara,

VICE (2015)
documentary, homework

pigtails, ribbons, long socks
Hello Kitty slippers
They advertise on flyers;
fortune telling, massage, walking
If you fold a 1000 paper cranes

you will be granted a wish.

in underwear

61

she's working, she told me,
as a lap dancer in Liverpool.
I, 28, saw Sarah in B&M Bargains,
pushing a pram full of bags;
the baby is in care

but she still got to keep
the little girl.

in Japan. $30 for 30 minutes
a member of the United Nations
they sign autographs for fanboys
old pervert middle aged men
sex sells

the Rights of the Child
little girl

2.

in his file it says
the boy, Y, 14 was
removed from his
family after
sexual abuse

Mum's partner convicted
I supervise
Home Contact
wants to play
and sister, X, 6
in the article it says,
the subject, A, 8
was posed semi-nude
in over 2,000 Polaroids
for sale, cats, cream

like Balthus, I turn my gaze
on the young girl
I do this with
mother-eyes
not not nubile

I write
The Guitar Lesson (1936)
masculine mother
Mum, Y
the broken doll
          X sits her
legs splayed
she is wearing knickers
Mum does not
ask her to cover up

in the article it says,
the subject, A, 8
was posed semi-nude
in over 2,000 Polaroids
for sale, cats, cream

Y is removed from
the children's home
the *jeune fille* Fuck you
dress it up in French
an apple tree

the hidden cunts
upskirters, artists, hebephiles

X sits her
legs splayed
she is wearing knickers
Mum does not
ask her to cover up

in the Gargosian Gallery
the doctor's daughter
15, for paying a girl, 8
to kiss him under
the portrait unfinished

paedophilia runs like
oil paint in some families

3.

P, 15, has a boyfriend, 24? 34?, in Bolton   Who Is Rotherham Ringleader?
mum is a prostitute, suspect sister   grooming
is a prostitute, P is for   police black/blues and twos
We transport her every Friday and Saturday silence
alone   1,510 more survivors

to see him, he buys her gifts   *you are the other girls*
she is less of a   *nymphet* *worthless, deserve to be*
risk   Risky Business (2011) Shhh-ut Up
of absconding. It's easier than having to   CPS turn the case down.
report another kid who's not come back to care.

Nazir Afzal, Pakistani Muslim, he is a small god, re-opened Pandora's rage
incompetence as young as 10 drugged drunk Asian daughters unreported *white cunts*
average sentence 13 years aye, me too, complicit in the car collect that sullen **Lolita**;
his phone, his music, his money *Mummy stop writing I want to introduce you to my friends*
online Star Stable do you have any time? some of them are American Ella Hill is a pseudonym

I don't know what happened to her.

abusers
they had mistaken for
friends and lovers

I'm a tramp, why would anybody

95% of the UK
sex offenders are
white males?

Hope crouches in a corner
believe me

Spoke 657: Requests for Prayers Welcome

St. Fishies had not been a church for years and years and years. It was in one of the History 'G' level modules. Local History. The government had bought it off the Catholics, listed it and left it pretty much empty. This is a hub and spokes model. Cycle. Cyclical. They occasionally had emergency walk-in medical stuff there. If the sky had fell bad and burnt loads of us. Or Vaxchora vaccines when the water went wine-coloured.

The module had directed us to walk over, sewted up obvs, to do some drawings and that. I couldn't work out if I was sick or excited going over on our own. Lola balancing on the cart tracks when she can, thinking she's a tight-rope walker. Me, on a lead, head down coz we walked past the spoke where we was evicted and I hate living in a lean.

Lola's Virgin Mary was pretty good. She drawn her 1960's style coz that was when the church was built. The actual one was real-sized in a plastic case outside the church. It were like some-thing in the doll museum. I creeped up to it slow coz I thought it might have a mech to make it move and fricking freak me out massive. Chalk pink skin, Disney princess hair and glass eyes, same colour as a chemical toilet.

Let's not even talk about mine. I give up and dabbed the windows on the church- abstract like. Orange, purple, blue. *You think you're Sophie Tauber-Arp.* Lola pointing at me and mi drawing, with her chewed pencil. *Shuddup, pencil dick* I sez back. Lola wets her knickers.

The best thing about it being listed was that the arc covered it properly, not one hole. Thanks Uncle Maintenance man. So when you got there, you could be outside, take your sewt off, instead of stinking B.O. sweating and use your real skin fingers to touch stuff. I touched all the granite walls. Lola bet she could climb them. *I bet we could climb up this, us. We could short the arc. Alice, we could. Frick things up a bit.* Funny bish. *You've seen too many climbing vids. You've no muscles and I'm a fat turd.* I wished we wuz rich and we had phones to take pics of everything and us at St. Fishies. Lola got 69% on her upload.

Spoke 657: Cheap and Cheerful

It was weird for me when she changed. Skins shed. I'd never known it. Her stripping herSORRYself a patch behind her ear. Pulling the hair out. One by one. And picking. Picking it behind her ear. Like she had mites or summat. *Ma. Stop picking. Please, Ma!*

If you carry on doing that, you stupid woman, Charlie, look at me, I'll handcuff you to the kitchen table. Eryk liked throwing his wa-wa-weight about. But she must have been doing it in her sleep. We kept catching her sobbing and shaking on the couch. Mewling. Mewling. Lola didn't know what to do. *When she's in this black place, I just make her cups of tea. And cuddle her. Even when she dunt cuddle back. Sometimes she'll drink em cold, if I just leave em.*

The weight dropped off her. Like a picture of an old woman. Lola tried to squeeze one of them high-fat avocado sachets down her. The posh ones. She proper slapped Lola hard. Ring ring. *What do you reckon we should do, Alice?*

Undone/Begun/Beg

re: Shamina/ Sharmeena/ Shamima Begum

My first thought, you made your bed. Lie in it.

I, 14, tell my Mum *it's a sleepover* fold a ~~baby~~ duvet like chapati in
a body-bag. I am in 94.68% white-Wigan. Mum is breast cancer
pink. My three friends are 14 too; Vickie, Shamina (unrelated),
Lauren, Kadiza, Amara and Marie. They aren't jackal enough
to doctor their ~~passports~~ duvets but take toothbrushes for their
sharp   ?puppy?   ?bitch?   teeth. We'll have to share
the hope I brought in the pissworn Grenfells of Manchester. I
want to sleep rough outside Mark Owen's house.

I hold on to Mum and *you don't belong here.*

The men think we are homeless and give us husbands. Lauren
is ashamed and wants to go home. Kadiza is killed in an airstrike.
Puke 20/20 vision down the stairwell. A good refugee Samaritan
on her way back from prayer in the nightclub brings us,
shivering, cups of tea from Bangladesh. I start to attend Bethnal
Green Mosque.

For two months Mum bobs, a balloon with raisin skin, until the
race-ribbon snaps. I, 12, stop listening to Take That or Rihanna or
my wicked step-mother. I spit out my Set 1 English in the park.
The women from the other mosque break into a taxi and take the
radio. I deactivate my ~~son~~ social media accounts.

Two years later. I, 14, tell my Grandmother a fairy tale *it's for
winter clothes* fold £500 into an origami Jesus. Get the bus ~~home~~

to ~~martyr~~ Istanbul/Raqqa/soon? My boyfriend buys me a kitten.
I marry a jackal. *It's a normal life but every now and then there are
bombs and stuff.* Wikipedia and The Telegraph are telling us my
mum died from cancer before the ISIS infection. Don't worry.
The BBC and The Mirror say my mum will take the 9 day old
baby and de-radicalise him.

Where is motherhood, in this?

Imperial Mother. Jarah is ~~dead~~ an innocent. Make an example
of a time you were not dangerous to the safety and security of
children living in this country. *I am cold.*

Let us lie and lie and lie. We made your bed.

Sell

The moon says Prince Andrew is the world's most protected N.O.N.C.E. #*metoo*

The Virgin Mary, 14, claimed she had been
driven to the mansion on El Brillo Way,
where a female_____ escorted
_____ pink-carpeted staircase,
then into _____ massage table,
an armoire _____ toys and
a photo of a little girl
pulling her underwear off.

Somehow I, 40, have learned
teach me, talking about S.E.X.
a form of foreplay.

Alice, 16: Before I say anything else …
um, is there a possibility
that I'm gonna have to
go to court or anything?

written by
a peach

Maureen Calaghan
New York Post
October 9 2016

Somehow I, adult me, mother me
learned that writing about sex
erotic literature.

Filthy Rich:
The Sex Scandal That
Undid Him
And All The Justice That

Alice, 16: Would you consider it rape, what he did?

Alice, 16: I don't want my family to find out about this...

'Cause Jeffrey's gonna get me. You guys realize that, right? ...I'm not safe now. I'm not safe.

Money Can Buy *she, 16, didn't know*
it was rape
written by
#notallmen James Patterson
John Connolly and Tim Malloy
2010

It's not your fault if
you're aroused.
It's the President's fault
It's the Pope's fault

It could be your fault
It's the Queen's fault
It's Jeffrey Epstein's fault
It's my mother's fault?

The brace blocks and wires should be a fricking electric fence, right? Delicious.
written by

me

Spoke 669: Fly Me to the Moon

The cellar door is open. Soft air. Salt cherry syrup crusting round the top. I listen to Lola 'n' Bert.

I like meeting you at night. I like how black it is. Like ink. I feel like a screwing ninja. Do you fancy mi Ma? I like you better than Eryk by a load. I like learning how to train the fancy rats. I like them running up my legs. Can I rattle the tin so they'll come looking for me? I feel safe with you Bert. I like how you don't talk that much. I like how you don't have screens down here. How did you get away with that? Wuz you in the Uprisings? I like having a secret.

They slaughtered the cats and dogs for drinking too much water and needing too much meat. This, before I were born. At first, the mass suicides were welcome too. Natural selection. Jump

jump jump. About face. The masses need comfort. Breed together the remaining stock. Cats + dogs = dats and cogs. Hairless as a plucked chicken. *You've never seen a plucked chicken, have you?* A few with Eyes mech-ed in. This kid, she's like a frickin puppy. *Tell your Mam you're coming here. She'll be thinking things.*

Don't think I've seen a chicken with its hair on, a shaved chicken or a chicken IRL.

Oh shuddup Bert, mi Ma won't think you're a paedo.

Spoke 657: Sixty Nine

Miss/Ms. Charlotte/ Charlize/ Charlie Daze.

Friday night is Charlize, pink and a bit sweaty, from making herself fricking gorgeous. Hair rolled and stacked like fairytale mattresses. Her full entire eye sockets dusty with a pot of *ethereal fuchsia* drifting up into her hairline. Her nuclear horizon look. She'd made loads from it. Well, enough to pay for two rooms in a unit in the slum spokes. Which is more than her Dad done. Lola helped her Ma give all the looks names. Charlotte had no Synth in her- genuine old-fashioned irl sponny looker.

Eryk's not coming again is he? Lola was practising her bored face/ bored voice so you couldn't tell how bothered she was. *Nah, I got some free credits for the Eroti-hub. Might as well use them.* Charlie was always trying to pull a security guard or an Uncle who could make stuff. What stuff? Stuff that is strictly legal, obviously.

The music was right up. She didn't give a screw. *They must pay teachers shocking coz he can't afford a cart to come over here. I thought it was good job.* Spontaneous eye roll. *He teaches us, Ma.*

POSTSCRIPT::

The following poems contain found text from news articles and interviews.
There is also reference to a line from a poem and the title of a song.
Please read and listen.

Page 3. SPOKE 657: ZERO
Garbutt, T. (2018). The Universe and Me. Hull: Wrecking Ball Press, p.8.

Page 8. ROUND 1
Baby, D. (1992). Let Me Be Your Fantasy. [Radio] London: Production House Records. Available at: https://www.youtube.com/watch?v=BWT-J2st1PpQ [Accessed 30 Aug. 2019].

Page 34.-36. THE HIDDEN
Tempesta, E. (2015). 'People think it's roleplaying. It's not: Documentary lifts the lid on the dark side of Japan's 'schoolgirl culture' and reveals how teen students are forced into prostitution by 'obsessive' older men. Mail Online. [online] Available at: https://www.dailymail.co.uk/femail/article-3168563/Documentary-lifts-lid-dark-Japan-s-schoolgirl-culture-reveals-teen-students-forced-prostitution-obsessive-older-men.html [Accessed 30 Aug. 2019].

Page 39. UNDONE/BEGUN/BEG
Read, C. (2019). Shamin Begum: Inside ISIS bride's 'NORMAL' life of bombs of severed heads in bins. Express. [online] Available at: https://www.express.co.uk/news/uk/1091530/shamima-Begum-isis-bride-syria-heads-bins-uk-citizenship-savid-javid [Accessed 30 Aug. 2019].

Page 40. SELL
Calaghan, M. (2016). The 'sex slave' scandal that exposed pedophile billionaire Jeffrey Epstein. New York Post. [online] Available at: https://nypost.com/2016/10/09/the-sex-slave-scandal-that-exposed-pedophile-billionaire-jeffrey-epstein/ [Accessed 30 Aug. 2019].

ACKNOWLEDGEMENTS

Private/s appeared in Peripheral Visions: Edge Hill Arcana, a commonplace curated and edited by Rebecca Sharp, (2019) Edge Hill University Press.

Second Sight, Spoke 657: Tom Cat, Playing Rounders, Scent, Quarry and *Spring* appeared as sound/film installation and sculpture in 'Love Is A Rebellious Bird' art exhibition, curated and re-imagined by AL + AL. 2 November 2019- 29 February 2020.

ABOUT VERVE POETRY PRESS

Verve Poetry Festival is a new press focussing intently on meeting a local need in Birmingham - a need for the vibrant poetry scene here in Brum to find a way to present itself to the poetry world via publication. Co-founded by Stuart Bartholomew and Amerah Saleh, it is publishing poets from all corners of the city - poets that represent the city's varied and energetic qualities and will communicate its many poetic stories.

Added to this is a colourful pamphlet series featuring poets who have previously performed at our sister festival - and a poetry show series which captures the magic of longer poetry performance pieces by poets such as Polarbear and Matt Abbott.

Like the festival, we will strive to think about poetry in inclusive ways and embrace the multiplicity of approaches towards this glorious art.

www.vervepoetrypress.com
@VervePoetryPres
mail@vervepoetrypress.com